SPOTLIGHT ON GEORGIA

GEORGIA DURING THE CIVIL WAR

SAM CROMPTON

PowerKiDS press.

NEW YORK

Published in 2018 by The Rosen Publishing Group, Inc.
29 East 21st Street, New York, NY 10010

Editor: Elizabeth Krajnik
Book Design: Rachel Rising

Photo Credits: Cover Stock Montage/Archive Photos/Getty Images; p. 4 Santi0103/Shutterstock.com; p. 5 The Cartoon Collector/Hulton Archive/Getty Images; p. 7 Interim Archives/Archive Photos/Getty Images; p. 8 https://en.wikipedia.org/wiki/Stephen_A._Douglas#/media/File:Hon._Stephen_A._Douglas,_Ill_-_NARA_-_528297.jpg; p. 9 MPI/Archive Photos/Getty Images; p. 11 Courtesy of Washington University (Saint Louis, Mo.) Department of Special Collections; pp.13, 19 Everett Historical/Shutterstock.com; p. 15 https://archive.org/details/constitutionalvi00lcstep; p. 15 (background) Reinhold Leitner/Shutterstock.com; p. 16 https://commons.wikimedia.org/wiki/File:Scott-anaconda.jpg; p. 17 https://commons.wikimedia.org/wiki/File:CSS_Atlanta.jpg; p. 21 (George H. Thomas) https://commons.wikimedia.org/wiki/File:George_Henry_Thomas_-_Brady-Handy.jpg; p. 21 https://upload.wikimedia.org/wikipedia/commons/d/d9/Chickamauga.jpg; p. 22 Courtesy of the Library of Congress; p. 23 Stringer/Archive Photos/Getty Images; p. 24 https://en.wikipedia.org/wiki/File:Savannah_Campaign.png; p. 25 https://en.wikipedia.org/wiki/Fort_McAllister_Historic_State_Park#/media/File:A_Sherman_Necktie,_Ft._McAllister._GA._US.jpg; p. 26 Courtesy of the Library of Congress; p. 27 Courtesy of the Library of Congress; p. 28 Courtesy of the Library of Congress; p. 29 Courtesy of the Library of Congress.

Cataloging-in-Publication Data
Names: Crompton, Sam.
Title: Georgia during the Civil War / Sam Crompton.
Description: New York : PowerKids Press, 2018. | Series: Spotlight on Georgia | Includes index.
Identifiers: ISBN 9781508159919 (pbk.) | ISBN 9781508159940 (library bound) | ISBN 9781508159926 (6 pack)
Subjects: LCSH: Georgia--History--Juvenile literature. | Georgia--History--Civil War, 1861-1865.
Classification: LCC E559.C76 2018 | DDC 975.8'03 --dc23

Manufactured in the United States of America

CPSIA Compliance Information: Batch #BS17PK For further information contact Rosen Publishing, New York, New York at 1-800-237-9932.

CONTENTS

CHAPTER ONE

THE BLOODIEST WAR

The American Civil War, which lasted from 1861 to 1865, was the bloodiest war fought in United States history. Many factors played a role in the start of this war. Many Northerners believed that Southerners were **immoral** for owning slaves. Many Southerners believed that the North had no business interfering in their economic and social existence.

Many people in the Southern states relied on slavery for their economic success. These people feared that laws passed by the Northern states and the federal government would lead to the end of slavery. Many white Georgians didn't own slaves, but in 1860, Georgia had more slaves than any other state except Virginia.

The North and South's disagreement over slavery caused 11 states, including Georgia, to secede, or break away, from the United States.

"NOT UP TO TIME;"

Or, Interference would be very Welcome.

This British political cartoon shows two slaves holding up President Abraham Lincoln (right) and Confederate President Jefferson Davis (left). In the background, the eagle and lion, which represent France and England respectively, discuss whether they should interfere in the war.

CHAPTER TWO

REACHING A COMPROMISE

The United States was expanding and the issue of whether new territories would allow slavery was **controversial**. Many Southerners believed in states' rights, meaning that each state could decide what was best for its residents. However, some Southern people only supported states' rights when the state chose to allow slavery. Some Southern legislators also believed that states had nullification rights. This means that they believed states could **nullify** federal laws they considered unconstitutional.

These disagreements about slavery seemed to be settled when Congress adopted the Compromise of 1850. This plan made California a free state, set Texas's borders, and allowed the new territories of Utah and New Mexico to choose whether to allow slavery.

The Compromise of 1850 was not a permanent fix. Georgia had its own idea for how to handle the debate on slavery.

Prior to the Compromise of 1850, the Missouri Compromise of 1820 tried to settle disagreements over slavery. It stated that slavery would be banned in all new states north of **latitude** 36°30′. New states south of that line would be able to decide whether or not slavery would be legal.

CHAPTER THREE

THE SOUTH CHOOSES SLAVERY

The Georgia Platform of 1850—a set of resolutions adopted by Georgia lawmakers—stated that Georgia would continue to follow the Compromise of 1850. However, it also said that Georgia would not tolerate any more of the federal government's attempts to interfere with slavery or ban its expansion. The Georgia Platform was credited with keeping the Union together—for a while.

STEPHEN A. DOUGLAS

In this political cartoon, Douglas (far left) and other American politicians force slavery down the throat of a Free-Soiler. Free-Soilers opposed the Kansas-Nebraska Act, which made it possible for slavery to spread throughout the western territories.

The Kansas-Nebraska Act in 1854 caused further problems regarding slavery. This act **repealed** the Missouri Compromise and allowed new territories joining the Union to decide whether or not they would allow slavery, a concept known as popular sovereignty. Stephen A. Douglas, a senator from Illinois and Abraham Lincoln's rival in the election of 1860, was a supporter of popular sovereignty. By the time Kansas achieved statehood in 1861, many Southern states had begun to secede from the Union and war was approaching.

CHAPTER FOUR

DRED SCOTT FIGHTS FOR FREEDOM

Throughout this time of disagreement in the United States, many slaves tried to gain their freedom. One of these slaves was Dred Scott. Scott first lived in Southern states where slavery was legal. However, one owner later took him to live in the North, where slavery was **prohibited**, before he returned to the South. After his master died in 1843, Scott tried to gain freedom for himself and his wife. However, his master's wife refused to accept his payment of $300.

In 1847, Scott took his case to court. After several lower court rulings, Scott and his lawyer decided to take the case to the U.S. Supreme Court. In 1857, the court decided that, because he was black, Scott was not a citizen of the United States and had no right to bring his case to court. The ruling outraged many U.S. citizens.

James Moore Wayne, one of the Supreme Court justices who ruled on the Dred Scott case, was from Georgia. The court ruled that black people had "no rights which any white man is bound to respect."

CHAPTER FIVE

THE ELECTION OF 1860 AND ITS CONSEQUENCES

In 1860, the Republican Party nominated Abraham Lincoln of Illinois as a presidential candidate. At this time, Lincoln was not yet a strong abolitionist. The Northern Democrats nominated Stephen A. Douglas, and the Southern Democrats nominated John C. Breckinridge. Yet another party, the Constitutional Union Party, nominated John Bell. This four-way race made 1860 a very exciting election year.

Lincoln did very little campaigning. His main goal was to present the Republican Party as a unified body. He believed that this unity could help him win the presidency.

On Election Day, Lincoln led the race. He won the election and, thanks to the common use of the **telegraph**, the news spread all over the country quicker than ever before. Most Northerners were pleased, but the majority of Southerners were unhappy. They believed Lincoln would try to end slavery right away. Southern states prepared to secede from the Union.

Abraham Lincoln won the presidential election of 1860 with over 1.8 million popular votes. Most of his votes came from Northern states.

CHAPTER SIX

THE DEBATE ON SECESSION IN GEORGIA

In December 1860, South Carolina became the first state to secede from the Union. Georgia was the fifth state to do so. In both states, **delegates** attended political **conventions** to determine the will of the people.

Many of Georgia's counties were divided. Immediate secessionists wanted to secede from the Union right away and never look back. Cooperationists hoped that Georgia would delay seceding by compromising with the Union. Despite some people's wishes, Georgia officially left the Union and joined the Confederacy on January 19, 1861.

The Confederate government was established first in Montgomery, Alabama, and then in Richmond, Virginia. Alexander Stephens was one of Georgia's leaders at the time of secession. He later served as vice president of the Confederacy. Stephens and several other Georgia legislators gave a strongly Georgian flavor to the new Confederate government.

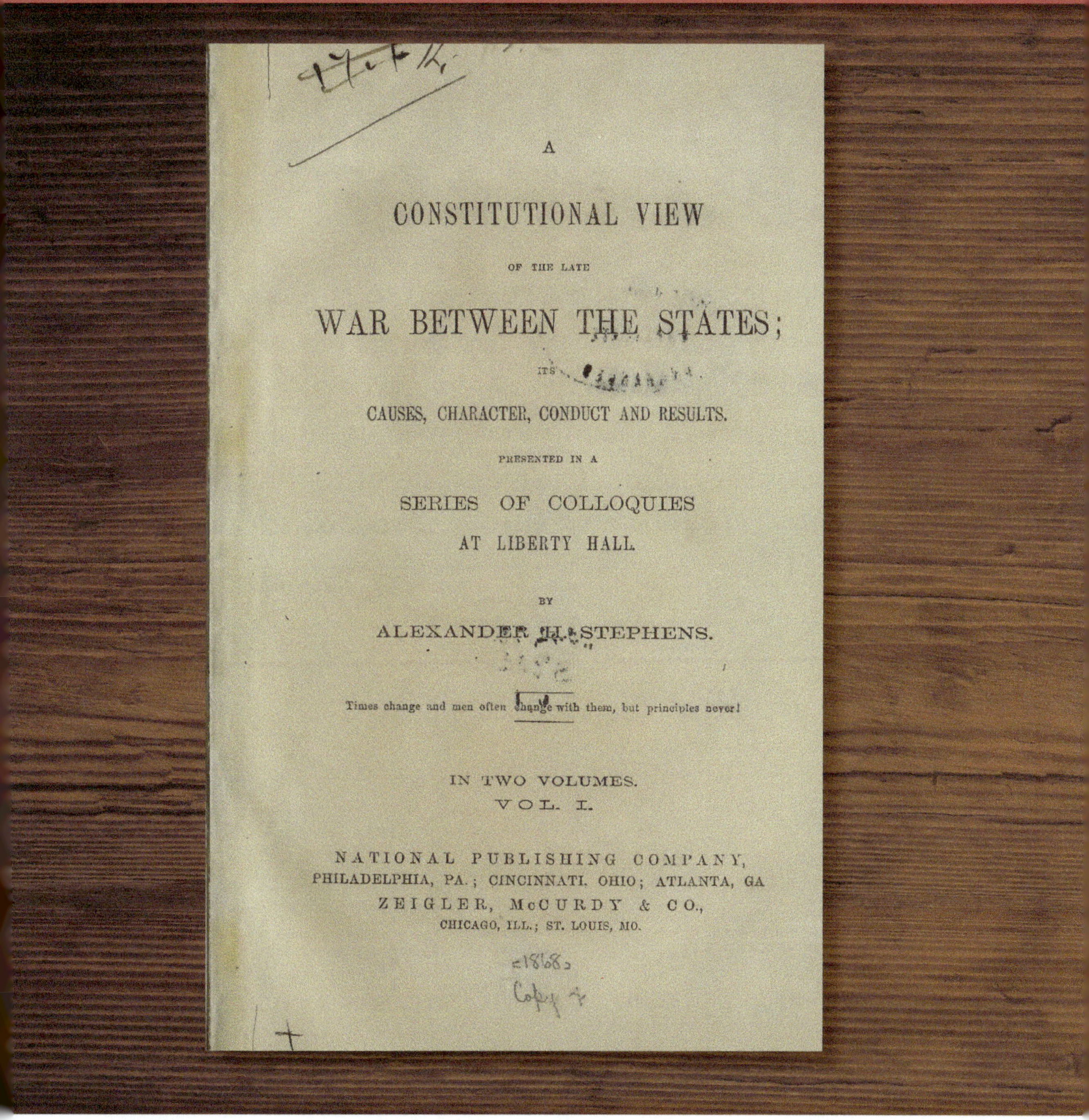

A

CONSTITUTIONAL VIEW

OF THE LATE

WAR BETWEEN THE STATES;

ITS

CAUSES, CHARACTER, CONDUCT AND RESULTS.

PRESENTED IN A

SERIES OF COLLOQUIES

AT LIBERTY HALL.

BY

ALEXANDER H. STEPHENS.

Times change and men often change with them, but principles never!

IN TWO VOLUMES.

VOL. I.

NATIONAL PUBLISHING COMPANY,
PHILADELPHIA, PA.; CINCINNATI, OHIO; ATLANTA, GA
ZEIGLER, McCURDY & CO.,
CHICAGO, ILL.; ST. LOUIS, MO.

Alexander Stephens was governor of Georgia from 1882 to 1883. He wrote a book, *A Constitutional View of the Late War Between the States*, about the South's viewpoint on states' rights and secession.

CHAPTER SEVEN

THE UNION BLOCKADE

The Union took several **precautions** to prevent the Confederate army from becoming too powerful. One **tactic** the Union used was a naval blockade, or barrier of ships, to stop the Confederates from importing military supplies and exporting goods like cotton. The blockade surrounded the entire southern coastline and controlled the Mississippi River.

The Confederates used gunboats to try to break the Union blockade at Savannah. These included the **ironclads** CSS *Atlanta, Georgia,* and *Savannah*. Although the Confederates used torpedoes to try to defeat the Union forces, the Union eventually gained complete control of the coastline.

This tactic was called the "Anaconda Plan" because it aimed to suffocate, or cut off, the Confederates' supplies.

The major port in Georgia at the time was Savannah. Many people attempted to break through the Union blockade to aid the Confederates. Edward C. Anderson of Savannah was the first person to sneak through the blockade on November 11, 1861. Anderson was transporting military supplies with his ship, the *Fingal*.

The Confederates tried to break the blockade. They attacked the blockade ships but could not break through due to the strength of the Union navy.

CHAPTER EIGHT

THE EMANCIPATION PROCLAMATION

The Union had larger armies and better-supplied soldiers than the Confederate army. The Union won several important victories in 1862. Perhaps the most important was the Battle of Antietam, fought in Maryland in September.

Just days after the Battle of Antietam, President Lincoln issued the Emancipation Proclamation. The proclamation declared that if all the Confederate states did not return to the Union, all slaves living in those states would be free as of January 1, 1863. Lincoln issued the Emancipation Proclamation without Congress's permission.

White Southerners were angry. They did not wish to lose what they thought of as their property. White Georgians declared that the proclamation would never be enforced within their state. However, slaves in Georgia were very pleased. They became more interested in the outcome of the war. If the Union won the war, they'd finally be free.

The Emancipation Proclamation did not automatically free slaves. Emancipation was a process that lasted for years. Emancipation wasn't truly achieved until enough states **ratified** the 13th Amendment.

CHAPTER NINE

THE BATTLE OF CHICKAMAUGA

Chattanooga, Tennessee, was an important city during the Civil War. This city was a major railroad center and the Confederate and Union armies struggled to gain control of it. Braxton Bragg and the Army of Tennessee gathered in Chickamauga, Georgia, 12 miles (19.3 km) southwest of Chattanooga, to attack General William Rosecrans's Union troops. Those troops had pushed the Confederates out of Chattanooga earlier that month.

On September 19 and 20, 1863, Bragg and his army attacked the Union forces with help from General James Longstreet and his troops. Major General George H. Thomas, known as "The Rock of Chickamauga," brought the Union forces back together after one of Longstreet's attacks and held onto the Union's position long enough for the Union troops to retreat.

The Battle of Chickamauga was a Confederate victory. However, Rosecrans and his Union soldiers still occupied the city of Chattanooga.

Thomas was very knowledgeable about military tactics. He earned his nickname from his actions during the Battle of Chickamauga, during which he was said to be standing like a rock.

CHAPTER TEN

SHERMAN'S WARFARE

Union Major General William T. Sherman used a new type of warfare. His goal was to defeat the Confederate forces both physically and mentally in order to destroy their will to fight. Sherman wanted to show the Confederates that the longer they fought the Union, the more they would suffer.

MAJOR GENERAL WILLIAM T. SHERMAN

The battle of Jonesboro, Georgia, was Sherman's last assault on the Confederate forces before his troops entered Atlanta. His tactics are still used by U.S. military leaders. Sherman is considered the American father of total warfare.

Sherman battled the Confederates for control of Atlanta, which was one of Georgia's most **prosperous** economic centers. The two armies exchanged attacks in the landscape surrounding Atlanta for four months. Sherman cut off all the railroad supply lines to Atlanta to starve out the Confederate troops, who abandoned the city on September 1, 1864.

Sherman's Atlanta campaign resulted in destroyed railroad lines, acres of burnt land, and parts of Georgia in ruins. Although his methods of warfare were harsh, Sherman's goal was to end the war swiftly with as few lives lost as possible.

CHAPTER ELEVEN

MARCHING TO THE SEA

Sherman did not want to remain in Atlanta. Instead, his goal was to continue crushing the Confederate army. In order to move all his troops, he cut his supply line. This meant that he and his entire army had to live off what was readily available from Georgia's fertile farmland.

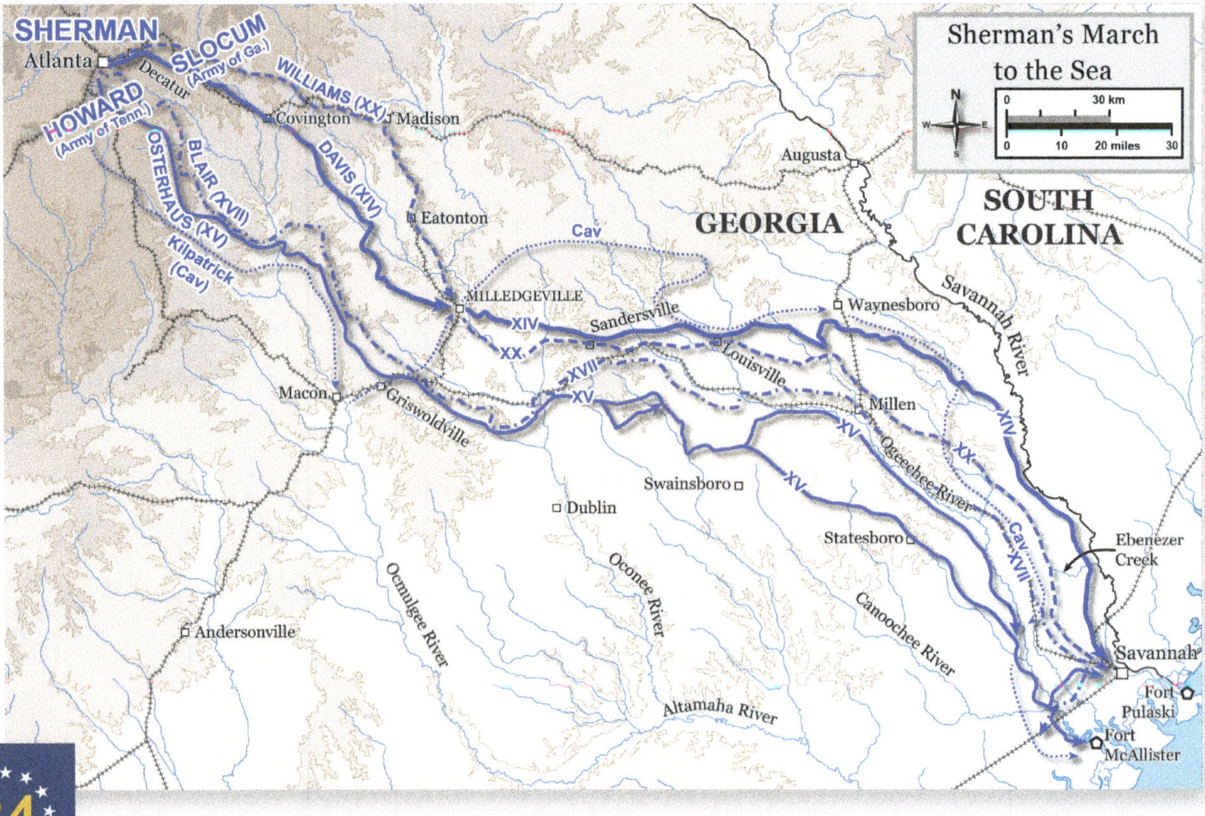

Sherman and his men caused a large amount of destruction along their path to the Georgia coast, but very few lives were lost. Sherman instructed his men to tear railroad rails from their ties, heat the steel, and twist the metal around tree trunks. These were referred to as "Sherman's neckties."

He moved the army out of Atlanta in four different groups of soldiers on November 15, 1864. Each of these groups took a slightly different path to the city of Savannah, Georgia. To keep his plans a secret, General Sherman cut down telegraph wires and didn't tell many people—including his superiors and his soldiers—what was going on.

Sherman's march to the sea ended on December 21, 1864, when he and his troops took Savannah. The city was a Christmas gift to President Lincoln.

CHAPTER TWELVE

PRISONERS OF WAR

Camp Sumter at Andersonville, Georgia, housed one of the largest Confederate military prisons of the Civil War. Created to hold Union soldiers, Camp Sumter turned into a place of terror. More than 45,000 soldiers were imprisoned there over time, and close to 13,000 of them died due to the horrible conditions. This overcrowded prison housed wounded soldiers who had little access to clean water, shelter, or food. Many of them suffered from different diseases.

Prisoners in Andersonville suffered terrible treatment. Prisoners did not have sufficient food, water, or shelter. Many of them died and those that survived were very unwell.

The prison was only meant to hold 10,000 soldiers at one time. However, at its most crowded, the prison held over 32,000 soldiers. The commander of the prison, Henry Wirz, was arrested after General Robert E. Lee surrendered to Ulysses S. Grant at Appomattox, Virginia. Wirz was later put to death for the crimes he committed during the war.

CHAPTER THIRTEEN

THE FIGHTING ENDS

On April 9, 1865, General Robert E. Lee surrendered to Union forces at Appomattox Court House in Appomattox County, Virginia. The war did not end immediately. However, this event was the first of many that marked the end of the Civil War.

JEFFERSON DAVIS

When Davis attempted to flee from Union troops, he threw on his wife's overcoat, which sparked rumors that he had tried to escape his captors by wearing women's clothing. This drawing depicts his escape as it was rumored to have happened.

One of the last battles of the Civil War took place on April 16, 1865, in Georgia. The battle of Columbus, Georgia, was part of Wilson's Raid, a series of attacks throughout Georgia and Alabama led by Union major general James Harrison Wilson. Wilson arrested Georgia's governor, Joseph E. Brown, and a number of Georgia's other leaders.

Wilson's capture of Confederate president Jefferson Davis in Irwinville, Georgia, on May 10, 1865, was one step closer to ending the war entirely. Shortly thereafter, Southern slaves were freed through the ratification of the 13th Amendment. However, the fight for equality was far from over.

CHAPTER FOURTEEN

TIME TO REBUILD

The Civil War was, by far, the most significant event in Georgia's history. The state's people were deeply affected by the war and the demands made upon them. Many of Georgia's men were lost in battle, leaving wives widowed and children fatherless.

While the South put up a strong fight, its people soon learned that the longer they struggled against the Union, the more destruction and death would befall them. Sherman's march through Georgia was **devastating** for the state. Whole towns, even counties, took years to recover.

Abraham Lincoln didn't live to see the very end of the war. A Confederate supporter killed him on April 15, 1865. But Lincoln's aim to reunify the Union was ultimately successful. Although Georgia was hesitant to ratify the 13th Amendment, which abolished slavery, the amendment became part of the U.S. Constitution on December 18, 1865. The slaves were now free.

GLOSSARY

controversial (kahn-truh-VUR-shul) Likely to give rise to disagreement.

convention (kuhn-VEN-shun) A large meeting of people for a common purpose.

delegate (DEH-lih-geht) A person who is sent to a meeting or convention to represent others.

devastate (DEH-vuh-stayt) To destroy much or most of something.

immoral (ih-MOR-uhl) Not following generally accepted principles of right and wrong.

ironclad (EYE-urn-klad) An armored naval vessel, especially one of the mid– to late 19th century.

latitude (LAA-tuh-tood) An imaginary line that runs east and west above or below the equator.

nullify (NUH-lih-fy) To cause something to lose its value or to have no effect.

precaution (pre-KAW-shun) Something that is done to prevent harm or trouble from happening in the future.

prohibit (pro-HIH-buht) To say that something is not allowed.

prosperous (PRAHS-puh-ruhs) Having success, often by making a lot of money.

ratify (RA-tuh-fy) To give legal approval to something.

repeal (rih-PEEL) To do away with, especially by legislative action.

tactic (TAK-tik) An action that is planned and used to reach a certain goal.

telegraph (TEH-luh-graf) An old-fashioned system of sending messages over long distances by using wires and electrical signals.

INDEX

PRIMARY SOURCE LIST

Page 23
The battle of Jonesboro, Georgia, Sept. 1, 1864. Lithograph. Created by Currier & Ives in 1864. Now kept at the Library of Congress Prints and Photographs Division, Washington, D.C.

Page 26
Andersonville prison. Georgia. Illustration. Created ca. September 28, 1865. Now kept at the Library of Congress Prints and Photographs Division, Washington, D.C.

Page 28
Jefferson Davis. Photographic print. Created between 1861 and 1865. Now kept at the Library of Congress Prints and Photographs Division, Washington, D.C.

WEBSITES

Due to the changing nature of Internet links, PowerKids Press has developed an online list of websites related to the subject of this book. This site is updated regularly. Please use this link to access the list: www.powerkidslinks.com/soga/civwar